YOUR
NOSE and EARS

Joan Iveson-Iveson

Illustrated by Bill Donohoe

The Bookwright Press
New York · 1986

All About You

Your Eyes
Your Hands and Feet
Your Health
Your Nose and Ears
Your Skin and Hair
Your Teeth

Acknowledgments

Sally and Richard Greenhill, p.5, 8, 19, 20, 21, 22, 23; J. Merrett, p.11, 12, 14, 16; Bruce Coleman Ltd (Jane Burton) p.17.

First published in the United States in 1986 by
The Bookwright Press
387 Park Avenue South
New York, NY 10016

First published in 1985 by Wayland (Publishers) Limited
61 Western Road, Hove, East Sussex BN3 1JD, England
© 1985 Wayland (Publishers) Limited

ISBN 0–531–18042–5
Library of Congress Catalog Card Number: 85–71729

Phototypeset by Kalligraphics Limited, Redhill, Surrey
Printed in Italy by G. Canale and C.S.p.A., Turin

Contents

What are they for?

Every day of our lives there are lots of new things to see, to smell, to hear, to touch and to taste. We take them all for granted, unless one of our five **senses** is missing.

Hearing and smelling are two very important senses. Without them you would live in a silent world, unable to enjoy all the different sounds and smells there are.

Your nose and ears are very important for two other reasons that you probably never think about. You breathe through your nose, and your ears help you to keep your balance. Although the boy in the picture is using his arms to steady himself, he would wobble even more if his ears weren't working.

Your nose

Look in the mirror at your nose. It might be short and turned up, long, thin, fat, or even hooked in shape. This is the outside part of your nose. It protects the openings to the air passages, and therefore your sense of smell. These two girls have different shaped noses.

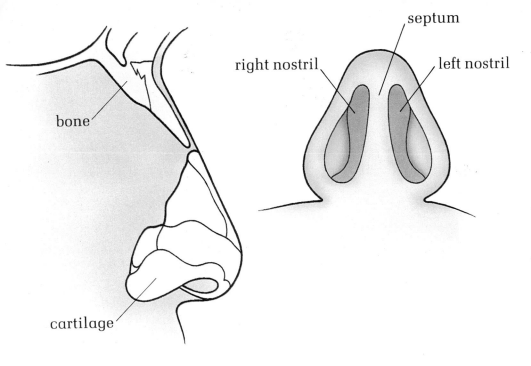

If you feel your nose, you will find that only the upper part is hard bone. The rest is a tough material called cartilage which you can easily move around.

The inside of your nose is hollow. The two **nostrils** are separated by a wall called the septum. The space inside your nose is lined with a special material, called the mucous membrane. This is sticky and covered in tiny hairs called cilia. It looks like a field of grass under a **microscope**.

Breathing

You do not have to think about breathing, you do it automatically. The air is sucked in through your nostrils and down into your **lungs**. The cilia trap the very, very tiny bits of dust and dirt in the air.

Inside your nose there are a lot of small **blood vessels**, all carrying warm blood. These warm the air before it goes down into your lungs. The boy in the picture is learning how to breathe without swallowing any water while swimming.

When you have a cold you sometimes find it very hard to breathe. This is because the lining of your nose swells, making the air passages smaller. You have to keep sniffing and blowing your nose to clear the air passages.

You sneeze a lot when you have a cold. You also sneeze when something is irritating the inside of your nose, like dust or **pollen**, so you create a blast of air to blow it out. A really big sneeze can reach a force of 60 miles per hour!

Your sense of smell

To smell something clearly, you sniff. This pulls the air carrying the smell up to the top of your nose. Here, there is a small patch of special **nerve cells**, as you can see in this picture. They send signals about the smell along a big nerve to the brain. Your brain then tells you what they mean. It could be your favorite food cooking, or a smell that means danger, like something burning.

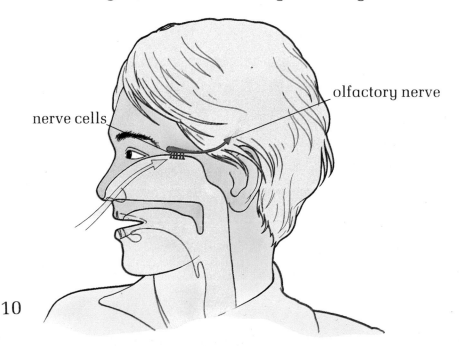

olfactory nerve

nerve cells

When you have a cold you'll find that you can't taste, or smell things very well. Your sense of smell strengthens your sense of taste, and while you have a cold the areas of your nose that pick up smells are covered with **mucus**.

To see how this works, try putting a piece of raw carrot, raw onion and raw potato on your tongue, while holding your nose. You'll find that it is impossible to tell the difference among them.

Taking care of your nose

Your sense of smell is very precious to you, which is a good reason to take care of your nose. The girl in the picture has a bad cold, and is blowing her nose. You should always blow your nose carefully. Close one nostril and blow through the other; never blow through both together, and never blow hard because you might make your nose bleed.

Don't pick your nose or stick anything up your nostrils. You might damage the lining of your nose and cause bleeding. You might even get something stuck.

Be careful when you are taking part in sports, and wear any protective equipment that is necessary. A blow on the nose from a baseball could break it.

If you have a nosebleed, do not blow your nose. Pinch it gently and lean forward. The bleeding will not take long to stop.

Your ear

Like noses, ears can be different shapes and
sizes too. The part that you can see when you
look in the mirror is shaped so that it collects
sound waves. It is called the pinna. The girl
in the picture is cupping her hand round her
ear to make a larger area to collect the sound
waves. This will help her to hear better.

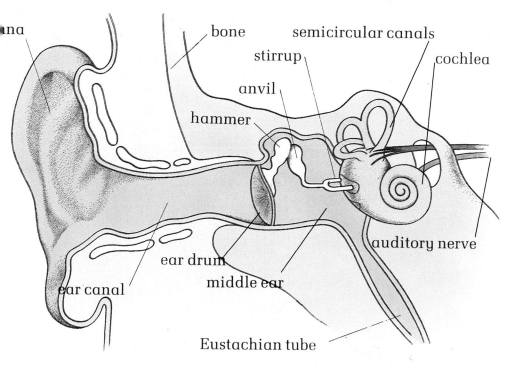

bone · semicircular canals · stirrup · cochlea · anvil · hammer · na · ear drum · auditory nerve · ear canal · middle ear · Eustachian tube

This drawing shows what the inside of your ear looks like. The ear canal leads to the **middle ear** which is sealed by the **eardrum** at one end. At the other end is the **Eustachian tube**, which leads to the throat. Inside the middle ear there are three small bones, the **hammer**, the **anvil** and the **stirrup**.

Inside the **inner ear** is the **cochlea**. This is shaped like a snail's shell, about the size of a pea. The auditory nerve takes information received by the cochlea to the brain.

Hearing

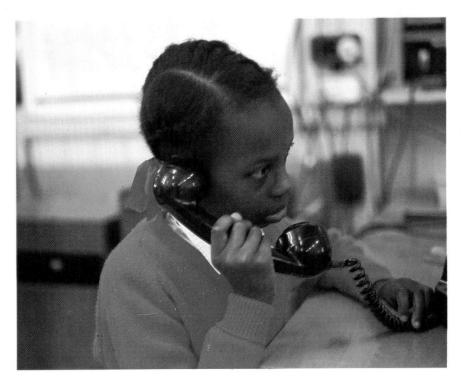

Hearing starts with your outer ear. Sound waves travel through the air and are collected by the pinna, which funnels them down a tube to the eardrum. The sound waves make the eardrum **vibrate**. This vibration is carried through the hammer, anvil and stirrup to the

inner ear. The nerves inside the cochlea receive the vibrations and pass on the information along the **auditory nerve** to the brain. The brain then sorts out the signals it receives.

It is not always easy for you to tell where a sound is coming from. Because you have one ear on each side of your head, you can tell where it is coming from only if you move your head. Animals, like this rabbit, are much better able to sense the direction of a sound, because they can swivel their ears.

Balance

Without your ears it would be difficult to keep your balance. Your brain is told which way up you are, whether you are going backward or forward or turning in circles, not only by your eyes and muscles but also by the semi-circular canals in your inner ear. The drawing shows you what these look like.

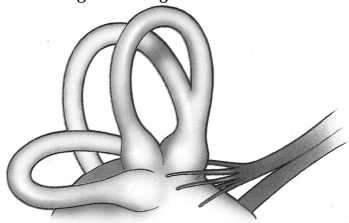

There are three canals, at right angles to each other, which are lined with fine hairs and filled with liquid. When you move your head the liquid rushes through the canals,

moving the hairs around. Nerves send this information to the brain. If you were about to fall over, your brain would send messages to your muscles to stop the fall.

Sometimes you feel giddy when you get off a merry-go-round. This is because your brain is confused by the signals it is receiving. Your legs are standing still, but the liquid in your ears is still moving around.

Deafness

A deaf person either cannot hear at all or cannot hear all types of sound very well. Deafness is caused for several different reasons. Blockages like wax, or a small swelling, will stop the sound waves passing through the middle ear. Damage to the inner ear, through infection, keeps the messages from getting to the brain.

Hearing aids, like the one this girl is wearing, can help some kinds of deafness by

making all sounds much louder. Lip-reading is very useful, too. Try this out with friends. Block your ears with your fingers, then see if you can lip-read what they're saying.

When people are born totally deaf, it is very difficult for them to learn to speak. The two deaf children in this picture are learning to talk to each other using sign language.

Taking care of your ears

The most common ear infection is in the middle ear. This is caused by germs traveling up the Eustachian tube into the ear. If your ears hurt, you should go to your doctor. The doctor can examine your ears with a special instrument, which shines a light into your ear, as you can see in this picture.

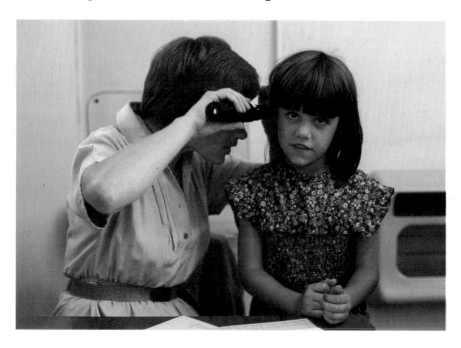

Sometimes ear wax hardens and blocks the ear canal. This makes you slightly deaf. A doctor can remove this for you. Don't try to do it yourself.

Don't put things in your ears. You might get something stuck or damage your eardrum.

Loud noises can damage your ears if you listen to them for a long time. People who work with noisy machinery should wear earmuffs to protect their ears.

Wear a woolly hat, or earmuffs, when the weather is cold, to protect your ears.

Glossary

Auditory nerve The big nerve that takes information from the inner ear to the brain.

Blood vessel A vein through which blood flows.

Eardrum A thin piece of skin in your ear, which is vibrated by sound waves entering your ear.

Eustachian tube The tube that leads from your ear to your throat.

Hammer, anvil, stirrup Three tiny bones in your ear which pass the vibrations from sound waves, from one to the other.

Inner ear The part of your ear that contains the semicircular canals and the cochlea.

Lungs The organs in your chest that fill up with air when you breathe in.

Microscope An instrument you look through to see tiny objects, which you could not see otherwise.

Middle ear The part of your ear that contains the hammer, anvil and stirrup.

Mucus A slimy liquid, which you get in your nose when you have a cold.

Nerve cells Areas where information is collected inside your body.

Nostrils The openings to your nose.

Pollen The dusty powder in the center of flowers.

Senses We have five senses, which are hearing, seeing, smelling, tasting, and touching.

Sound waves The form in which sound travels through the air.

Vibrate To tremble or shake rapidly.

Index